This book is dedicated to my children Ray"Drion, Daniel, Hannah, and Keara. A mother's love is priceless, and I love you with all my heart. May God bless you all to have a long life full of joy and happiness.

To all the single moms that are struggling to raise their children. God can see all things, and he knows every situation. Stay strong!

Inspired By the Father

By Amanda Matthews

Why I am Thankful

As I look around the classroom in my home I am in awe of what the Lord has done. It is His mighty power, and grace that has kept me over the years. I am thankful not because I am forced to, but because I am a very blessed and kept woman of God.

I know that I am nothing without the power of God. With Him I know that I can do all things and know that I have triumphantly succeeded in every battle that I have ever faced. With him I am more than a conqueror. I am a hero in my own right. Being a spiritual being made in the image of my Father, sets me up on a higher standard of living.

I thank God for the life that I live. I thank the Lord for his love, mercy, and grace. I may not have a mansion, but I thank God for the roof over my head. I may not own a limo, but I thank the Lord for the car that I drive. I may not wear designer clothes, but I thank the Lord for the clothes on my back. Most of all I thank the Lord for His Son that died on cross for my sake. It is my Father whom I give all the glory and praise. That is why I am thankful. I praise God for all that he has done.

Be of Good Cheer

I know that life can be hard sometimes, and it seems that no one understands the struggle. There may be days that you want to question why things are going wrong. You may be filled with doubt, and do not feel like smiling, but let me offer you some encouragement. There are a million reasons why you should be hopeful. Most important above all God loves you with an unconditional love. HE cares for you. If you are reading this then that means that you are very much alive and well. That is another reason that you should be happy. God has blessed you to be alive and among the living. You may not feel it, but you are worth all of the love that God has placed on the inside of you. It does not matter what you look like, or what your status may be WE are ALL children of GOD. Be of good cheer today and no that God loves you. Here is a scripture for you today. "These things I have spoken unto you that in me ye might have peace. In the world ye shall have tribulation: but be of good cheer; I have overcome the world." John 16:33

I hope that you will be blessed today. Remember that God loves you and so do I. Until next time may God bless you with peace and prosperity.

God's Perfect Timing

Hello everybody I hope that you are doing well on this beautiful day. God is just blessing me to do some great things in life. You know when I first started with the concept of a business idea; I was not sure what I really wanted to do. In my early years as a homemaker I had plenty of time to sit, and think of the type of business that I had wanted to invest my time in.

When my children were really small I had always known that I wanted to be home with them, and still have an income to take care of the household. For the last five years I have been eager to get started with my business plans, and have discovered that God has given me several visions when it comes to entrepreneurship. It has taken plenty of patience for me to get to this point. Let me give a scripture to those that might be struggling with patience. "And let us not lose heart in doing good, for in due time we shall reap if we do not grow weary" (Galatians 6:9)

Keep Dreaming

He race is not always won by going very fast. It is a fact that we should not procrastinate, but we should not expect everything to be spontaneous. God has everything set for his own timing, and he does everything in accordance to his plans for your life. Do not grow weak and weary, but wait on the Lord. Continue to do well, and you will reap a harvest for your work.

God will not lead you down a path of destruction, nor will he give you over to the enemy. God loves, gracious, wise, and he loves US with an unconditional love. Even when it comes to our dreams God is there. I am stepping put on faith and I am trusting God. He is involved in my relationships, my education, my relationships, in the rearing of my children, and all that is existent on this earth. (It is amazing what the Holy Spirit will do that message is for someone who will read this)

My business is designed for women. I will be selling jewelry, clothing, skin care products, and hair accessories. I am so excited about what God is getting ready to do. In the weeks to come I will be showing samples of the things that I will be offering. Stay tuned!! Until next time may God bless you with peace and prosperity.

Do Not Fear

I am excited about my business, and I am looking forward to bringing products that I know women will love. My business is for all women, but I founded the company with the single mother in mind. I know that some single mothers are not able to afford clothing and jewelry, because they are too busy providing for their children. "Afro by Design" is for the woman that wants to feel beautiful at affordable prices. I will be selling real African products. In the near future I will have dresses, necklaces, bracelets, earrings, and other items for women from all walks of life.

I have learned that we cannot be afraid to step out on faith, and trust the Lord to help us reach our destiny. It is His plans for our life that will come to pass as long as we trust in Him. There is a scripture that has to come to mind as I am writing this post. It says "Trust in the Lord with all your heart, and lean not unto your own understanding; in all your ways submit to him, and he will make your paths straight." (Proverbs 3:5-6)

Motherhood

Being a mother is more than just wearing a title
It is a calling
It is a job
It is a blessing
That is bestowed upon all women
It is more than just singing your children to sleep
It is more than just reading them stories at bedtime
What about the moments:
When your child was born
When he/she babbled his/her first words
What about the moment they walked for the first time
Or they had an accident on the playground
What about the first time you taught her how to ride her bike
Or you cheered them on at their soccer game
How about all the times that she was sick
And wanted you to hold her hand
And feed her chicken soup
You can remember every ceremony, ball game, dance, and
Everything that your child has done
You look for every smile
And every opportunity to be there for your children
You are blessed as a mother
I am blessed to be a mother

Proverbs 31:10

Choices and Christian Motherhood

When I look at the world that we live in I have to ask myself some questions. As a mother should I be strict on my children, or give them a little freedom? As a Christian parent should I allow the kids to watch all cartoons? Do certain celebrities have an impact on my children's lives? These are just a few of the questions that I ask myself each day. As a mom what should I do?

With so much new technology children have a chance to access anything from any location. I think that media plays an important role in what children are viewing and hearing. With the click of a button they can see anything on the Internet. One touch of the remote and kids are looking at all kinds of music videos. Is this entire media really healthy for developing minds?

The other day my daughter was watching a music video of a very famous singer. She looked at me, and said she wanted to be just like her. Immediately I asked her what she liked about the singer. She said "Mommy the singer is beautiful, and she is rich." Okay there is nothing wrong with wanting to be beautiful and have money, or could that create a problem if I am trying to teach her about virtue.

Virtue

In Proverbs 31:30 it says that "Charm is deceptive, and beauty is fleeting; but a woman that fears the Lord is worthy to be praised." I want my daughters to know the true meaning of being a woman. I want to teach them the importance of a healthy body image, and their value in the eyes of the LORD.

Every parent is in a position to be a role model for their children. As a mom I am my children's first teacher, and role model. I am obligated to teach them the word of God, and help them develop. My daughters look up to me, and see me as the person that they want to be. I pray to God daily to help me be the best that I can be. I am an advocate for Christian based programming. I think that there is a need for more Christian shows for children. I pray that you have been touched by my blog. If it has touched you in any way please feel free to leave a comment and I invite you to follow. I believe that you will be blessed.

I am excited about what God is doing for me. The children are doing really well in school, and we are just praising God for our new beginnings. The children are getting a lesson on life. I am giving the children seeds and flower pots.

It is never too late to make a Change

I believe that it is never too late to make a new start in life. Even in the most difficult situations you can pick yourself up, and start moving again. It is amazing after a storm, like a tornado some people still have the courage to rebuild everything that they lost in the storm. In my case after my divorce I had to literally pick up the pieces, and start my life over. In the beginning it was very overwhelming, because I had four small children that were depending on me to take care of them. We all know that storms can be very devastating, but when you know that you are a survivor, you feel an overflow of blessings. The challenges that I have had in my life has helped me realize how strong I am, or how strong that I have become. I believe that life's challenges prepare you for a blessing, or can make you better and stronger.

He is God All of the Time

I am a single woman of God raising four kids on my own. I wear many hats, and I know that I am sustained by God's mercy and grace. I am a mother, writer, psalmist, and the first teacher to my children. I thank God for the guidance of the Holy Spirit, and I will always seek the face of my Father first. There is one thing that I have found to be a fact. GOD will never leave nor forsake you, and HE loves All of His children more than anything in his world.

No matter what you have been through, or what you are going through God is always there for you. Storms do not last always, and God is a refuge in a time of a storm. I hope and pray that you are having a good day.

Lord Thank You

Lord I am asking

Let my light shine today

Let someone be blessed

Transformed

Inspired

Changed

Let them see you in me

Let their hearts be glad

Let them rejoice in your glorious presence

I pray that every man

Woman

Boy and girl be blessed

They will prosper and do all things

Through our Lord Jesus Christ

They will be all that God has called them to be Lord we worship

you

God We Give you Praise

We give you all the praise

We bow down to you

Oh your holy name Jehovah

Glory to God

For He is so holy

Thank you Jesus

Thank you Father

El Shaddai we worship you

WE thank you.

The Lord is The Light

Greetings everyone I hope that God is blessing you with peace and prosperity. You know I really love this time of year. I love watching the seasons change. The trees are displaying all kinds of colors. This is the time of year where the kids and I get a chance to decorate the yard with pumpkins, fall flowers, and other decor. WE sit in the yard enjoying the cool breeze, and taking long walks in the park. As we look at the month of October there is a newness of the month that is fast approaching. That means that a change of the seasons is near. This is the first day of autumn, and the beginning of a new season. I am writing this as my children are engaged in their work. Our classroom is really quiet, and it is very easy to focus on my writing. Through homeschooling we are learning more about each other. I have four children, and they all have different learning styles and it makes teaching them very interesting. I have tried different techniques, and ways of teaching multiple subjects. My styles of teaching have seemed to work for all four learning styles.

I can never write a post without mentioning a scripture. In this case my scripture has everything to do with children, and biblical holiness. I am not perfect, and I do not claim to know everything, but I do live my life based on what the Bible says. 2 Timothy 3:16-17 says "**Scripture is breathed out by God and profitable for teaching, for reproof, for correction, and for training in righteousness, that the man of God may be competent equipped for every day work.** "

As a parent I love to be involved with my kids. These are my rules of engagement. We pray together as a family every morning. We learn with and from each other. We take our knowledge from the Bible, and I am teaching how they can apply this knowledge to their lives, and we have fun together. Doing things with my children is one of the most important parts of my day.

Training Your Children

 I am a firm believer that children should be taught in the way that they shall go. I teach my children based on the principles of Proverbs 22:6 is says "Train up a child in the way he should go, and when he is old he will not part from it."
Each parent is different, but the most important factor is raising children effectively. As a mom I train my girls to cook, clean, sew, and iron. Well some may say that is a little old fashioned, but they are women in training. One day they will have a family of their own, and they will need to know the basics of housekeeping. My sons are learning the same lessons, but in a different perspective. All parents have a set of values, and beliefs that they want to instill in their children. My beliefs are in close relation to the Bible. My children are being trained, and prepared for life. I thank God that he has bestowed this blessing on me. In the near future I will have my non-profit organization up and running. My mission/ministry is to teach young girls their value and worth in the eyes of God and the world. Until next time may the Lord bless you with peace and prosperity.

There is No Need to Be Afraid

In the past few weeks I have been talking about my business, and what I want to offer women from all walks of life. I have placed so much trust in God to help me make things happen, and I am confident that God will supply all the resources and provisions for this business to come to pass. With every post I like to add a scripture that is very beneficial to what I am creating. In the book of Habakkuk 2:2 it says "Write down the revelation and make it plain on tablets so that the herald may run with it." (New International Version)

To me this is more than a business; it is a part of my ministry. I have always felt the calling to help and encourage single mothers. As a child I was a part of a single parent home, and I had seen firsthand the things that my mother had to experience. And now that I am a single mother of four, I have experienced the highs and lows of single motherhood.

When I think of all the things that I want to bring to girls and women, I think of simplicity in an elegant form of fashion. Jewelry that has been hand crafted in Africa. I will be selling dresses of vibrant colors, and hair accessories that can accentuate a woman's personal style. There will be earrings and bracelets that can be added to any outfit. There will be hair accessories that will perfect any hairstyle.

Dream Big

- If you continue to wait for your dreams to come true, do you think that life will pass you by?
- If you allow the opinions of other people to mold your character, do you believe in yourself?
- If you are sitting around depressed and worrying about life, do you trust God?
- If you died today where will you spend eternity?

Life is a very precious commodity, and I am grateful for the life that God has given to me. I want to do more than just exist. I want to make a difference, and give my life more meaning. With just a little bit of creativity I can help change the life of a child. A simple coloring book can lift the spirits of a sick child. Kind words of encouragement can give a teenager hope, and prayer can change the lives of people all over the world. You don't need to be a scholar, or a star to help someone in need. A little can go a long way. This is my year to bless the lives of others. I may not have much, but I have enough to give to someone that has less than I do.

She is a Mother

There are moments with my children that are priceless
There are times when I am so overjoyed to be a mother
To hear the sounds of tiny footsteps running through the house
To hear their voices when they cry
The proud feeling you get
To know that you are a leader with authority
The calm position of being a nurturer
The fact that you are a beacon of light
The high calling that God has called you to
The blessing that was bestowed upon all women
There is the fact you forget all the pain of labor
But you know that you have power and strength to carry life
You do not care about awards
Or want to be mother of the year
My joy comes from the laughter of my children
Their voices
Sweet
Precious
Loving and joyful
A mother is so many things
She is a
Teacher
Mentor
Trainer
Coach
Friend
Minister
Nurturer
Most of all
She is a woman of God
Designed to teach her children about God and life

She is Special in the Sight of The Lord

A long time ago I had the pleasure of meeting a young lady who had suffered from low self-esteem and depression. She had multiple talent, and very exceptional. Like most young women I know she could not see what God had created in her. She believed that her physical beauty was more important than what was on the inside.

For years she had been tormented, and teased for what she looked like. What she had experienced left her with emotional scars, and made her feel less valuable. There are so many young girls that are suffering from low self-esteem, low self-confidence, and a low opinion of themselves.

As a teen I had issues with depression and low self-esteem. Thank. GOD I realized who I was in him. I love the Lord, and I know that I am a child of God and the righteousness of Christ. I wish more young women knew that they are more valuable than silver and gold.

GOD loves you and so do I. I am comfortable with the skin that I am in. God made each one of us special, unique, and designed for a purpose.

My Help Comes from the Lord

There is a scripture in the Bible that says "I look to the hills where my help comes from my help comes from the Lord." In my eyes that scripture has so much meaning and it is very close to my heart. I cannot tell you how many times that I have contemplated on this scripture and it has spoken to my heart. In this life I have had some storms that have spiraled out of control, yet I could always count on God to be a refuge in the time of those storms. I have learned that God is the same yesterday, today, and forever. He will not change no matter what the season is.

I have also developed a mindset that exudes nothing but positive thoughts. I have decided to make positive affirmations every day that God blesses me with. I have made up my mind that I will not live with a defeated mentality. I believe that as a child of God, and a believer I can be victorious in every situation. 1 Corinthians 15:57 says "But thanks be to God, who gives us the victory through our Lord Jesus Christ" We do not have to be defeated by the enemy. It is the enemy that comes to kill and to steal and destroy, but Jesus has come to bring life more abundantly.

We can be confident in knowing that we can do all things through Christ. He is our strength, and we can trust what the Lord has said.

Jesus is the Best Gift

For unto us a King is born in the city of Bethlehem. He lay in the manger next to his mother Mary. All have come to adore this sweet child by bringing him gifts. There was a star shining in the night that symbolized the birth of the Messiah. We honor our Lord and Savior Jesus Christ for he is the reason for the season.

Jesus Christ has given his life for us to be free. 2 Corinthians 8:9 says "For you know the grace of our Lord Jesus Christ that though he was rich; yet for your sakes he became poor so that you through his poverty might become rich." Those that have not are rich through our Lord Jesus Christ. He, the Son of God did not have a place to lay his head. Luke 9:58 says "Foxes have holes, and the birds of the air have nests, but the Son of man has no place to lay his head."

Jesus lived a simple life, and he was very open with the people. He was not conceited even though he knew that he was royalty. I love Jesus, because he gave himself for all mankind. He does not discriminate, or show favoritism. His love is unconditional, and he gives his love freely. Even though most of society has taken God out of almost everything he is still on the throne. You may try to take Christ out of Christmas, but he still lives. He is more alive now than he was in the past.

Great Expectations

With each passing day all of my hope is renewed. I have great expectations about each new day that God has given to me. The past is behind me, and is nothing more than a memory. My mind is set on my goals, and focused on the future before me. I have always known that God had plans for my life. Jeremiah 29:11 says "For I know the plans that I have for you, declares the Lord, plans to prosper you and not to harm you, plans to give you hope and a future." Hallelujah, God wants me to prosper, and he will order my footsteps in His Word!!! Psalms 119:133 says "Direct my footsteps according to your word; let no sin rule over me." God has plans for each of us, and he wants all of us to prosper in life.

This year I am on fire with the word, and I am on fire for Jesus. I am asking the Lord to let me walk in more love. I want him to create in me a clean heart. In Ezekiel 36:26 God said "I will give you a new heart and put a new spirit in you." I thank the Lord that he can transform me from the inside out. God has the power to remind me that the past is gone, and all things are now new. 2 Corinthians 5:17 says Therefore if anyone is in Christ, the new creation has come. The old is gone and the new is here." There is newness in this season. That is something to be glad about.

Trust

We cannot forget everything in the past, but this is our chance to start over, and wipe the slate clean. With the New Year in full swing some of us have trouble letting go of the past. I am a witness that some things are not easily forgotten, but I thank God that what has happen is over. Those events in life have made me stronger, and appreciate what is in my future. We have to forget what is behind us in order to move forward. Philippians 3:13 says "Brothers and sisters I do not consider myself yet to have taken hold of it. But one thing I do; forgetting what is behind and straining for what is ahead."

Each day is new, and a beginning to bring about change in your life. I have to make constant changes in order to reach my goals. Lamentations 3:22-24 says "Because of the Lord's great love we are not consumed. For his compassions never fail." God is always in the throne. Thank God that I can start over and begin again. This is a new season and another opportunity for me to prosper.

The Cure for the Blues

You know this time of year can be tough for singles. I have seen many people get depressed just because they want to be in a loving relationship. When you think about it, the holiday season is full of expressions of love, family, and all types of joy. There are many reasons why people are single; it could be the death of a loved one, or separation and divorce. Many of us singles have found it to be extremely hard to happy this time of year. When you are hurting there are some people that will not relate to what you are feeling. There may be a myriad of things that may distract you from seeking God.

The kids are home from school and they are extra active, you have bills that need to be paid, and you don't have the money. You want to buy Christmas presents, but you have to buy food for the house. I have been there. In the past I had so many reasons why I was depressed. I would throw myself a pity party, because I was divorced. I would sit, and remember all the things that hurt me. I constantly reminded myself of all the things that happened. One day I made up my mind to change my situation.

I had to learn that God was the source of all that I needed. It was His love that has sustained me through the tough times. It was His light that was shining in the dark places of my life. Instead of feelings depressed I had to learn to get involved. B e an active participant in this thing called life. If you have children create joy for them. You should be an active part of their lives. Know that you can lean on God for those moments of loneliness and depression. This holiday season can be a happy time and you can enjoy it. Remember that God is only a prayer away, and you deserve to be happy!! Until next time may the Lord bless you with peace and prosperity.

Godly or Worldly Standards

This week I will be talking about acceptance. I have noticed that many young women want to serve God, and live by the standards of the world. The fact is God is calling us to live by a higher standard of life. Society has glamorized certain lifestyles, and many young people feel like they should be included in it. Most of them feel that being popular is better than having morals and values.

Can we live by the world's standards, and still please God? The Bible says in Romans 12:2 "Do not conform to the pattern of this world, but be transformed by the renewing of your mind. Then you will be able to test and approve what God's will is—his good, pleasing and perfect will." As Christians we should live a life that is pleasing to the Lord. We are made in the image of God, and we are representatives of our Father. That means that everything we do is being reflected, and the world is looking at us. We are examples to the world. Matthew 5:14 says "You are the light of the world. A town built on a hill cannot be hidden." As Christians we are to be set apart, consecrated, and separate from worldly standards. Even as young Christians we need to be mindful of everything that we think, say and do.

Thank God for Youth

Being young is not an excuse not to serve God properly. In fact it can be a very powerful statement. I often tell my children that living for God and representing Him in their generation can be a very powerful statement. It can also be a very powerful form of expression. With so much darkness in this generation they can let their lights shine in the darkness of their generation. (Yes children can be beacons of light)

I am convinced that many young girls believe that less is more. Most of them have been led to believe that less clothing is more attractive. I cannot and will not blame society for everything, but the world has glamorized the cliché that less is more. The truth of the matter lies in my ability as a mother. I have two daughters, and I have an obligation to teach them respect for their bodies. For the Bible says in 1 Corinthians 6:19-20 "Do you not know that your bodies are temples of the Holy Spirit, who is in you, whom you have received from God? You are not your own; you were bought at a price. Therefore honor God with your bodies." It is meant for us to honor our bodies and respect it.

This week the children are learning about the importance of godly standards, and what God requires of us. They understand the concepts of both godly and worldly standards, and must learn to differentiate the differences between the two of them. We are also getting ready for the holidays, in which we are always thankful to the Lord for all that he has done.

An Attitude of Gratitude

Even in the midst of a problem (No matter how bad it looks) you can depend on God to see you through. It may seem hard to trust Him, but know that He has everything in His power and control. For a brief moment I thought that I would never see my children again, but my faith in God kept me strong during a moment of weakness.

I have an attitude of gratitude, because I know that the Lord keeps an eye over me and my family. I have to give a big thanks to the children's bus driver for her act of bravery. She is being honored today for what she has done for the eleven students that was being held hostage on that bus.

Thankful

In some parts of the world many people are dying. The very things that we may take for granted are the things that someone else may need to survive. Something like a plate of food, or a cup of water could change the life of a person. I was watching television last night, and I saw a commercial that touched my heart. A group of small children were huddled around water well. They were holding cups waiting for a glass of fresh water. I could tell that they were thirsty, and in need of a cool drink. The missionary said that some people walk seven miles just to obtain water for that day.

I thank God for providing all of my needs, and I pray that he will provide for them as well.

Blessed are those who have regard for the weak
The Lord delivers them in times of trouble
The Lord protects and preserves them
They are counted among the blessed of the land
He does not give them over to the desires of their foes
The Lord sustains them on their sick bed
And restores them from their illness. Psalms 41:1-3

I pray that the Lord will provide the needs of all His children. My prayer is that all little children will have a warm place to stay, clean water, and something to eat.

I know that there are times in your life that you simply don't know what to do. You constantly look for ways to ease the pain that you are feeling. You forgot that today would have been your 15th anniversary, but you divorced several years ago. Friends and family do not seem to understand why you have not remarried, or at least dated a little. You want to get out and mingle, but you are terrified of loving someone again, in fear that he/she may hurt you. The children insist that you get out of the house to go watch a movie, but you are consumed with the idea that you have to take care of them 24/7. It is hard for you to let go of the idea that the kids are getting older, and you can relax a little bit.

It is around nine in the morning, and you have been contemplating about your life, you have examined every inch of yourself, and every aspect of yourself. You have looked up and down for a solution, and have felt the anxiety of what you have been thinking. It seems like there is no way out. The government shutdown has got you feeling stressed. The way of the world has you feeling blue. The fact that you haven't met the right guy has you wondering of love still exist for you. You are concerned about the kids futures...........relax and breathe.

God will not leave you in a situation without providing a way out. The Bible says in the book of Philippians 4:6 " Be anxious for nothing, but in everything by prayer and supplication, with thanksgiving, let your requests be made known to God." You do not have to live your life in turmoil, or suffer from anxiety. God has everything lined up in his perfect will for your life. No matter what is going in in the world you can be in perfect peace. Philippians 4:7 says "and the peace of God, which surpasses all understanding, will guard your hearts and minds through Christ Jesus." In Jesus we can have perfect peace, be at rest to enjoy life. It is true that life is not a bed of roses, and tests and trials will come, but as children of the Most High God we can find solutions to every problem.

When you leave your request with God, know that he has heard your prayer. Some results are instant, and others may take time to come to pass. He is God, and He knows what you are in need of even before you utter the words. God is able...... he is God... and He knows YOU. Take a deep breath, and relax. Everything will be alright. Until next time may God bless you with peace and prosperity.

HOPE AND PRAY

Dear child

Why are you weeping?

I want to dry your tears

You do not have to cry

I am here

To be your comfort

Have faith and believe

Believe that I will help you

My Father sent me

So that you could live

Your days in good health

With longevity of life

Come to me and find peace

Have hope and pray

God will answer you

He cares for you love

Have hope and pray

Jesus

Believe in what God has said

May your sleep be peaceful?

When you go to bed

May your dreams be sweet with grace?

May a smile be upon your face?

The entire world

Is his glory

I will tell you about his story

Born to a virgin named Mary

Son of the Most high

Lord of the worlds

Son of perfection

A light of the earth

He is God

Sinless

Perfect from the birth

A friend

A brother

A father and a mother

A Confident Woman

A confident woman knows

That she is made in the image of God

She is the light of the world

She can dance and she knows

That God is in control

She can shine her light

In the darkest places

She is the queen of her home

She is a mother

Wife

Sister

Teacher

Preacher

Lover

Worker

And she is the daughter

Of the Most High God

I am a confident woman

The Bridges That I Build

Shall I burn the bridges that has been built

I will wait on the Lord

For he has the power to change all things

Behold his glory

Behold the power of the Lord

His grace and mercy endures forever

I bow down to the power

Of the almighty God

Feelings of elation

Knowing that I have come from the Lord

I know who I am

And I love the Lord

With all that is in me

He is A Prayer Away

He is just a prayer a way
He does not discriminate against me for the color of my skin.
He is not concerned about my clothes
Or the way I wear my hair
He is not bothered about what I have watched on T.V
Or who I talked to
God is not concerned about how much money I have
Or how many degrees I have earned
He does not care about the car I drive
Or the type of house that I live in
I am glad that he is in love with me
And He is concerned about me as a person
He loves me unconditionally
Where would I be?
If Jesus had not come and died on the cross
There is no greater love
Than the one that He provides for me

No is no greater love than the love of God. There are no barriers that can keep me from His love. God is love and He cares for ALL of His children. There is no one that is omitted from this love, and we can always depend on the assurance of God's love. We should not fear, or be afraid of anything when it comes to the love of God. God heals, and he saves. I will always say that I have a joy and a love that the world did not give to me. Yeshua Christ our Lord and Savior has done it all for me. It is His love that has set me free. All my praise and love goes to God, the lover of my soul. Until next time may God bless you with peace and prosperity.

God's Blessing

I am a child of God. God gave me destiny before I was
born. While I was in my mother's womb God had a plan for my
life. Even though I have fallen short of the glory of God he still
loves me. While I lay in the pits of hell he extended his hand of
mercy to me. When the people decided that they wanted to
persecute me God came to my rescue. He has brought me to a
place of refuge. When my friends left me, and they turned their
backs on me God did not forsake me. Nor did he let me
down. When the money was low God provided me food, clothing,
and shelter. When the bills were due, and nobody would loan me a
dime God provided me with money. For every pain that I felt God
the Lord blessed with me with comfort, and he showed me
love. God is number one in my life. He is the reason that I exist. I
love the Lord. He is the Lily of the valley. It is time for the
women of God to stand up, and take back our children. Our
children are dying. They are in trouble. Half of our youth will die
before the age of 21. It is more likely for the young men to die of
violence. The young ladies in this generation will die of AIDS,
and domestic violence.

I Will Choose Life

I give glory to God for all the love that he has given to me. The
good Lord allowed me to see a new year. I thank the Lord for that
entire he has done in the past, and what he is getting ready to do in
the future. He has blessed my four beautiful children to be healthy,
and full of life.
From the first moment I knew that I was pregnant the Lord was
with me. Early in my pregnancy I had trouble with diabetes and
high blood pressure. Despite what the enemy tried to bring my
way I gave birth to my son. He was born two months early, and he
stayed in the hospital for two weeks. Today he is autistic, and one
of the smartest little boys I have ever seen. I gave birth to three
other children. I have hope that all my children will grow under
the authority of our Lord and Savior Jesus Christ. Today I have
chosen life. God has promised everlasting life. A life with God is
worth it all. And the fact that he has blessed me to live in his
grace. I hope that the Lord will bless you with a prosperous
year. Know that the children are the future. We can see that they
are the leaders of tomorrow. I love the LORD! He has blessed me
to have joy, peace and love.

Coming Out In Grace

The lord has shown me favor
He has saved me from the hands of the enemy
He has shown me love
He has brought me joy
He has blessed me to still live in his presence
I love the Lord
For all his mercy and tender love
Believe that he died for you to have everlasting life
He hanged on the cross for your sins
He has come to bring salvation to all that need peace
Blessed are the ones that cannot call out in the name of Jesus

He has come to bring peace and salvation to all that call upon his name. His name is Jesus Christ, and he loves you so much. Until next time may the Lord bless you with peace and prosperity. I invite you to listen to my mini podcast, and my gospel song located right here on my blog page. Thank you and God bless. If you would like a copy of my newsletter subscribe by email, and I will email you the most recent copy free of charge.

Prayer Can Change Things

I believe there is power in prayer. As I continue to delve deeper in my study of prayer and meditation I am learning many new things about the power of prayer. Prayer is my time where I can communicate with God, and listen to his voice. It is within the moment of prayer that I have discovered how powerful it is. It is more than just a simple conversation, or a time to ask for help. Prayer is my time to converse and commune with my Father.

During prayer I am in the presence of God, and I have a sense of peace as I pray. The Holy Spirit has taught me many aspects of prayer, and I have found that prayer in beneficial in my life as a Christian. As I continue to walk with God I am in awe of the power that He has. My time with God is very precious, and I look forward to communing with Him on a daily basis. "And pray in the Spirit on all occasions with all kinds of prayers and requests. With this in mind, be alert and always keep on praying for the entire Lord's people." (Ephesians 6:18) One of the most important lessons that I am teaching my children is how to pray. They have a very good understanding of how important it is to have a relationship with God, and how to pray. We pray as a family, and use that time to just give reverence to God. I will never underestimate the power of prayer, and will always believe what the WORD says about it. "Do not be anxious about anything, but in every situation, by prayer and petition, with thanksgiving, present your requests to God. And the peace of God, which transcends all understanding, will guard your hearts and your minds in Christ Jesus." (Philippians 4:6-7)

There is power and peace in prayer. My prayer and hope is that you will be well and have happiness and joy on this day. Jesus died on the cross so that we could have life more abundantly. God is worthy of all our praise all of the time.

God Has It in His Hands

God has all things under control
He has the world in the palm of his hands
Even when you are not sure about life
God has got it
You can be assured
That he will supply all of your needs
He will help you in every situation
And you know that he has got it
When you don't have money to pay your bills
When you do not feel well in your body
When you have trouble on the job
Do not worry
God has got it!!
Be thankful unto the Lord
Have a heart of gladness
Have an attitude of gratitude
Because the Lord has got it
He loves you
He wants you to prosper
He wants you to be well
He wants you to trust in Him
Do not worry
Do not fret
The Lord has got it!!

"Do not fret because of those evil
Or be envious of those who do wrong;
For like the grass they will soon wither,
Like green plants they will soon die away.
Trust in the LORD and do well;
Dwell in the land and enjoy safe pasture.
Take delight in the LORD,
And he will give you the desires of your heart.
Commit your way to the LORD;
Trust in him and he will do this:
He will make your righteous reward shine like the dawn,
Your vindication is like the noonday sun.
Be still before the LORD

Keep Your Plans in Focus

-
  If you continue to wait for your dreams to come true, do you think that life will pass you by?

- If you allow the opinions of other people to mold your character, do you believe in yourself?
- If you are sitting around depressed and worrying about life, do you trust God?
- If you died today where will you spend eternity?

Life is a very precious commodity, and I am grateful for the life that God has given to me. I want to do more than just exist. I want to make a difference, and give my life more meaning. With just a little bit of creativity I can help change the life of a child. A simple coloring book can lift the spirits of a sick child. Kind words of encouragement can give a teenager hope, and prayer can change the lives of people all over the world. You don't need to be a scholar, or a star to help someone in need. A little can go a long way. This is my year to bless the lives of others. I may not have much, but I have enough to give to someone that has less than I do.

I will trust God to lead me the right way, and I will never stop believing in myself. If there is anyone that does not know Jesus Christ I pray that he will come into your heart.   Our children are in need of change. They need to know who Jesus is, and they need to be saved as well. My ministry is designed to give hope, motivation, and encouragement.   Please join me on September 26th to pray for all children. They really need our prayers. We all have gifts and a purpose.

On Eagle's Wings

High above the clouds
There is a place that I love to soar
Eagle's wings
Taking flight
Into the sky
I can look beyond what is below me
Deep down in the pits of the valley
I can soar high in the sky
On eagle's wings
Like a bird
I will take flight
I will fly so high beyond the clouds
I will spread my wings and fly
Like a bird
I will take flight

But those who hope in the LORD will renew their strength.
They will soar on wings like eagles; they will run and not
grow weary, they will walk and not be faint" Isaiah 40:31

In every situation we can find a way to look beyond our
circumstances. God always provides a way out of every
circumstance, and we can trust in Him to help us with the
solution to our problems. Keep soaring high above all the
bad things that can occur in life

Inspiration

I would like to take a moment to thank the Lord for such a beautiful week. It has been an amazing journey. This week was very productive, and I had a chance to get plenty of work done. The kids and I had a chance to hang out, and watch television. We had a long lesson on Ephesians 6:1-2, and a list of academic lessons. They learned about the importance of prayer, and being kind to other people. Every week I try to emphasis the importance of a good attitude, and having good manners.

As I was sitting in my back yard I had a chance to just breathe in the fresh air. Despite the fact that the south really heats up this time of year, I had a moment just to see all of the beauty that God created. I am not talking about nothing that is man-made, but the things that God created, I had a chance to gaze at the trees, and look at the clouds in the sky. I looked at the beautiful green grass, and realized how blessed I am.

When I see my children playing outside their laughter melts my heart, and places a smile on my face. I said "Ms. Amanda, you are a blessed woman." It is very inspiring to see my children happy and free without any worries, and that is how I am feeling right now. I am happy, joyous, and full of laughter. My kids and I we have this great connection with each other. We seem to have fun no matter what we are doing. Today was our family day, and we just enjoyed watching some of our favorite animated programs. My daughter Hannah made us a batch of cookies

Before I go I would like to leave you with a word of encouragement. God has a plan and purpose for all of our lives. HE has created each of us for a purpose. God did not create anyone that is insignificant, and He believes that <u>ALL</u> of us are worthy. No matter who you are God loves you, and so do I. Smile you are somebody in your own unique way.

Faith

Faith is the substance of all things hoped for, and we can have hope in Christ Jesus. I have never seen God forsaken the righteous, or have known the Lord to forsake His children. In my own life I can be a witness to how good God has been to me. God has loved me, and been there for me through some difficult times. There are no barriers that can keep us from the love of God. He is always present for those who need Him. All my hope is in the Lord, and I know that he will never let me down. God is not like a man that he shall lie, and you can believe in what God says. It is written in His Word. Philippians 4:19 says "And my God will meet all of your needs according to His glorious riches in Christ Jesus." Praise God for His mercy and grace!!

Psalm 31:24 "Be strong and take heart, all you who hope in the Lord"

Psalm 39:7 "But now Lord, what do I look for? My hope is in you."

Lamentations 3:24 "I say to myself, The Lord is my portion, therefore I will wait for Him."

Romans 8:25 "But if we hope for what we do not have yet, we wait for it patiently."

I Speak Life

Do not give up on your dreams. God has a plan for all of us. Most people are afraid to dream big, and allow fear to take control. One of the greatest mistakes I could make is giving up on my dream. The devil wants us to quit and give up. He wants us to be quiet, and have no hope in God.

By the power of Jesus Christ I can do all things. If God is for me then who can be against me? I am the righteousness of God, and made in His image. I am destined to be a winner, and my Father is my Rock of salvation. God is El Shaddai, and he is Jehovah Jireh. He is the Great I am, and the Prince of Peace. With a Father like that why should we fear? Jehovah Shammah is good all of the time. I will continue to rise, because God has a plan for me.

There is life and death in the power of the tongue. Every word that you speak has the power to harm or help you. Your spoken word can determine your future. Whatever you speak will be manifested in your life. I have made it a habit to speak positive things in my life. I trust God, and I have faith in my Father. I can trust and believe that God will see me through every situation, and He is able in all things, He is Jehovah Jirah.

I Believe In Me

Okay I have decided to go into business for myself, and will be self-publishing all of my books, poetry, and literary works. I have been a freelance writer for the last eighteen years, and I love what I do. During my journey I have found that my writing has become more meaningful. As I think about my relationship with God, I have become a little more intimate with my gifts that he has given to me.

Sometimes what I write is more than just words, and I am sincere about everything that I say. My writing is a platform for me to share the Word of God with people, and tell how good HE is to me and my family. God had given me the vision for a writing business about ten years ago when I was much younger. At the time my first son was very young, and I was doing freelance writing while I was home with him. In the past I have had mentors that have guided me on the journey of writing, and I love them so much for all of their insights. I have been going through a process to make these visions a reality. I know that all things have been possible through God, and His spirit has been guiding me through this process.

My Life's Design

Yesterday I was looking out of my living room window, and I heard a conversation that my daughter Hannah was having with a friend. Apparently the friend was not being very nice to her mom, and I heard Hannah tell her about the scriptures that she is learning this week. This week I am teaching from the scriptures of Ephesians 6:1-2.
She told her friend "As children we should obey our parents". I had to thank God that she had been listening with such a great intent. Out of curiosity I had to ask the other children about this week's lesson. I was very pleased to know that all of them had remembered the scriptures. I do not claim to be the best mother, but I am always overjoyed that my parenting is not in vain.

Each mother has her own way of teaching her children, and their methods may be different from mine. What is so unique is we all share the responsibilities of motherhood. Because I have so much respect for being a mommy I have decided to take my writing to the next level. I am getting ready to step out on faith, and trust God with all that I have. All of my hope is in the Lord, and I know that He will be faithful as I walk on this journey. God is not like man that He shall lie, and I trust Him to the fullest. I am getting ready to combine my literary ministry and business together. I know that this is my season, and I am super excited. There have been a few delays in my new book being released, but I believe that it will be worth the wait. I think that it is so powerful when we find our own voices. I have found my voice, and thank the Lord for all that he is doing in my life, business, and ministry. I have learned that it is good to rest during the process, so that you can have the strength to handle your purpose in God. Motherhood, Writing, Singing, and Ministry are all a part of my life. This is my life and my calling. God is so good. Until next time may the Lord bless you with peace and prosperity.

My Life as a Single Mom

As a single mother I have so many things that I have to do, and I have to think about my own well-being. I have to make sure that every area of my life is in order. I work really hard to make sure that my children get what they need. I am involved in their education. I try to be at every school function, activity, and be involved in their lives. I have a very close relationship with each one of them, and love them very much. I just realized that I need to take care of me. In the mist of raising my children, and providing for them, I have discovered that I need some rejuvenation. That is where my prayer life and the Word of God come into the light. I have found that meditating on the Word of God and prayer helps me to stay focused. Life as a single mother can have its moments of stress and challenges, but I have managed to keep everything in line. I have always thought I would get depressed, but God has been a beacon of light, and has loved me through this process.

I have decided to make some changes in my life, and transform myself from the inside out. As I continue to go through the healing process, and develop my character, I know that God is walking with me. As a Christian woman I have decided to live a life of celibacy, and wait on the Lord to send me the right man. I have heard that love is better the second time around. All my hope is in the Lord, and he has been my strength. I am looking forward to my new beginnings, and each day is an opportunity to do something new. When life has its uncertainties we can always trust that God will be there. Until next time may the Lord bless you with peace and prosperity.

Holy God

Lord, you are majestic, and I praise your Holy name today. Words cannot describe the love that I feel for you. I owe you everything for what you done on the cross. Nothing but your blood will cover me all the days of my life, and I will always have a testimony in my mouth, Because you love me I have a song in my heart that I will sing for all eternity. I have a dance of praise because of you. I have an everlasting joy that this world cannot take away. You are the light of my life, and the joy of my heart, and I thank you Lord O I really thank you for all that you have done.

I sing because you live, and I sing because I am happy. Father God you alone are worthy of all my praise, and I will sing of your love forever.

Now if we died with Christ, we believe that we will also live with him. For we know that since Christ was raised from the dead, he cannot die again; death no longer has mastery over him. The death he died, he died to sin once for all; but the life he lives, and he lives to God. In the same way, count yourselves dead to sin but alive to God in Christ Jesus. Romans 6:8-11

Learning to Give

As a mommy I have always been keen on teaching my kids how to give without expecting anything in return. This week they will be giving toys to charity for other children to enjoy. I do not want them to be selfish, or have a selfish attitude about giving.

"Do not withhold good from those to whom it is due, when it is in your power to act." Proverbs 3:27

"But when you give to the needy, do not let your left hand know what your right hand is doing, [4]so that your giving may be in secret. Then your Father, who sees what is done in secret, will reward you." Matthew 6:3-4

I have always said that motherhood is a serious calling, and I am enjoying the experience of being a parent. Every week the children have lessons from the Bible. Each week we learn new scriptures, and I help them apply it to everyday life. Even though they are not perfect, I have been blessed with a good group of children, and they know mommy loves them.

Giving

Today my children and I have taken the time to be kind to the poor. There is great joy in helping someone who may need a little extra help. There was a mother that did not have food for her child, and a father that needed clothes for his son. I am a single mother, and I have had my portion of storms. Praise God he has lifted me from those dark days of lack. I want my kids to know the importance of having compassion for mankind, and how materialistic things can fade over time. They need to see how blessed they are to have all of their physiological needs met, and have some materialistic things to enjoy. The lessons that I am teaching them are not directly from society, but what I am teaching is filled with biblical principle. I have an obligation to instill them with the right things. The basis of what I am teaching is full of the Word, and has a vast amount of godly instruction.

I consider being a mother more than just a job. I believe that motherhood is one of the most important callings from God. Mothers are teachers, trainers, role models, and examples for their children. In the Bible Proverbs 22:6 says "Train a child in the way he should go, and when he is old he will not turn from it." In my case I believe in training my children with the Word of God. Preparing and teaching them with the scripture. Each mother has her own method of teaching her children, but she is a teacher to her children.

Part of my daily prayer is for God to help me be the best mother I can be, and guide me to make a major impact on this generation. Children are the future, and they need all the instruction, guidance, and training to be effective.
I also believe that children can be saved, and know the importance of salvation. My children know what Roman 10:9 means and they are aware of the sacrifice that Jesus made for us. Being a mom is one of the greatest blessings in my life, and children are the greatest gifts.

Jesus

As I sit here thinking about what the word says about the life of our Savior I realize that I can never repay him for all that he has done. I often wonder how Jesus felt about his life on this earth, and what he is thinking about how we are living today. We know from the scriptures that Jesus was born in a manger surrounded by animals. In the book of Luke 2:16 says "So they hurried off and found Mary and Joseph, and the baby who was lying in the manger." You would think that the King of the world would have been born in a better place, but he was born in a barn. The story of Jesus's life has always touched my heart, and brought an enormous amount of joy to my soul. To follow a man like Jesus is an honor. His life was very simple, yet it had great complexity. My Savior experienced what it is like to be human, and he is the Lord of Lords.

Do you ever think about how Jesus felt when Peter denied him? The Bible says that "Immediately the rooster crowed the second time. Then Peter remembered the words Jesus had spoken to him." "Before the rooster crows twice you will disown me three times." And he broke down and wept. Mark 14:72 the word says that Jesus knew that Judas would betray him. Matthew 26:14-16 says that "Then one of the twelve the one called Judas Iscariot went to the chief priests, and asked" what are you willing to give me if I hand him over to you? "So they counted out 30 silver coins. From then on Judas watched for an opportunity to hand him over. What a small price to pay for the life of the Messiah.
Can you see Jesus carrying a cross on his back? A crown of thorns placed on his head. People laughed and mocked Jesus. The Son of God was given vinegar to drink. "Immediately one of them ran and got a sponge. He filled it with wine vinegar, put it on a stick and offered it to Jesus to drink." Matthew 27:48 Oh my Lord it says that after this event Jesus cried out and he gave up his spirit. Matthew 27:50
Joy

The most important part of this story is not even death was able to keep Jesus. Jesus said in Matthew 27:63 "After three days I will rise again." What a reason to stand up and rejoice!

Joy

Joy is defined as a feeling of pleasure or happiness that comes from success, good fortune, or a sense of well-being or something that gives pleasure or happiness.

The joy that I have in my heart the world did not give it to me. My joy comes from knowing Jesus Christ as my Savior. Because of my relationship with Jesus I have an everlasting joy, and an everlasting love. When I gave my life to Jesus Christ I had a made up mind with the intent that I would serve him for the rest of my life. At an early age I had known about the sacrifice that Jesus Christ made for me. My joy has derived from the fact that nothing can replace the joy of the Lord.

Psalms 51:12 says "Restore to me the joy of your salvation and grant me a willing spirit to sustain me." It is the joy and peace of God that sustains me. Jesus Christ is my portion and my strength. I often tell my children that the materialistic things of this world cannot provide them with joy. It some cases it can, but it may be temporary. Nothing can provide more happiness than the love and joy of Jesus. I am also thankful for the blessings of being a mom, and able to help people.

My ministry is based on the fact that I love music, and the creative arts. "David told leaders of the Levites to appoint their fellow Levites as musicians to make a joyful sound with musical instruments, lyres, harps, and symbols." 1st Chronicles 15:16 A relationship with God is so beneficial. Psalms 16:11 says "You make known to me the path of life; you will fill me with joy in your presence, with eternal pleasures at your right hand."

Praise God for his joy and love. I will sing for God, and I will dance for God. I am a vessel waiting to be filled. Even in times of trouble we need to praise the Lord and have joy. When it seems like all hope is gone I know that God is able. Nothing is impossible for the Lord. This is Psalmist Amanda saying God bless you

Satisfied

For the times that I have been hungry
You have given me bread to eat
For the times that I have been thirsty
You have allowed me to drink from the living waters
When I was fearful and afraid
You have been there to comfort me
When I was lost in the wilderness
You have found me
When I have suffered from loneliness
You have been there to comfort me
When I was in need
You have provided for me
When I was sick
You were the one who healed my body
When I ask you for wisdom
You have given me the truth
When I was in need
You have come to my rescue
When I was crying
You have come to wipe away my tears
When I was angry
It was your strength that has kept me calm
When I need a friend
You are always there
When I needed saving
You sent your Son to die on the cross for me

Just Let God Handle It

Jesus answered "It is written, Man shall not live by bread alone but on every word that comes from the mouth of God." Matthew 4:4

"For God so loved the world that he gave His one and only Son that whoever believes in Him shall not perish but have everlasting life." John 3:16

Matthew 35:25-40
" For I was hungry and you gave me something to eat, I was thirsty and you gave me something to drink, I was a stranger and you invited me in, I needed clothes and you clothed me, I was sick and you looked after me, I was in prison and you came to visit me.'
"Then the righteous will answer him, 'Lord, when did we see you hungry and feed you, or thirsty and give you something to drink? When did we see you a stranger and invite you in or needing clothes and clothe you? When did we see you sick or in prison and go to visit you?'
"The King will reply, 'Truly I tell you, whatever you did for one of the least of these brothers and sisters of mine, you did for me."
(NIV)

Believe God

Has the doctor given you a bad report? Are you constantly suffering from anxiety, and worrying about life? Sometimes life can get a little out of control, and it can be overwhelming.

In the Bible Jesus says "Do not let your hearts be troubled." John 14:1 Not only can we believe in Jesus, but we can also smile or praise our way through any circumstance. When you read and meditate on the word of God it can bring you comfort and joy. Praying and talking to the Father can allow release of negative emotions. It can generate feelings of love, warmth, comfort, and elation of the spirit. Look at this scripture in the book of Isaiah 41:10 says "So do not fear, for I am with you; do not be dismayed, for I am your God. I will strengthen you and help you; I will uphold you with my righteous right hand." How comforting it is to hear these words from our loving Father. God is a refuge in a time of trouble.

I know that the storms of life can rage out of control, but as believers we have an advantage. Jesus Christ is our source of comfort. In the book of Matthew 11:28 it says "Come to me all you who are weary and burdened, and I will give your rest." HE said "Take my yoke upon you and learn from me, for I am gentle and humble in heart, and you will find rest for your weary souls. For my yoke is easy, and my burden is light." Jesus loves us so much that he does not want to see us suffer.

Praise God that Jesus Christ is my Savior. You can let go and let God handle that heavy load that you carry. We are not walking alone in any circumstance. God is with us every step of the way. He is there to comfort you when you cry. He understands all the pain, anxiety, heartache that you may be feeling. Because he loves us we have a reason to smile and (Praise) our way through anything.

Joel 2:21 says "Do not be afraid land of Judah; be glad and rejoice surely the Lord has done great things."
Psalm 69:30 says "I will sing God's name in song, and glorify him with thanksgiving."

Lord we thank you for all that you have done. Thank you for a willing mind, and an open heart. We know that challenges will come our way, but we have all confidence in YOU.

I Am

When I first came into the world
I had to take small steps
I had to learn how to crawl
Before I walked
God has always known
That I would stumble
He has always known that I would fall down
And try to walk again
He knows that the road will get rough
And the storms of life will rage
He knows that trials and setbacks
Will make me stronger
I will take small steps
Until I am able to walk
And then I may run
Until I reach my destiny

I am so blessed to be a mom. One of the greatest joys of being a mom is watching my kids develop. They all have unique personalities, and I am always encouraging them to be the best at everything. Sometimes parenting can be a tough job. What if you are single and parenting alone? I am a single parent of four beautiful children, and I have learned that this is one of the toughest jobs that I have done.

From the birth of my first son to the delivery of my youngest daughter, I have experienced some highs and lows in motherhood. The journey through motherhood has been a good one for me. I did not say that I have never had a moment of weakness. There have been times that the storms of life were raging out of control, and I needed to seek refuge under my Father's wings. The Bible says "God is our refuge and strength, an ever present help in trouble." (Psalm 46:1)

I have experienced days in the valley. I have searched all over the place looking for answers to my problems. I have spent many sleepless nights leaning towards my own thoughts. Scripture says "Trust in the Lord with all your heart, and lean not on your own understanding." (Proverbs 3:5)

I had to learn to trust in God with all of my thoughts. HE has been my daily bread and my comfort. For all the days that I feel like I have nowhere to turn; I can trust that God is always there for me. Because I trust him I have an assurance in His Word that he will be there. It says that God will never leave nor forsake me. That means that if all my friends and family leave me God is the one that will remain in my corner. Being a single mother raising Christian children is both rewarding and difficult, but through it all I know that I can depend on the LORD to help me through my hard times. "He is a father to the fatherless, a defender of widows, is God in His holy dwelling." (Psalm 68:5)

I cannot judge and condemn the man that says there is no God, but His presence in my life has filled me with the richness of joy and happiness. Because He is God I know that I am more than a conqueror, and a victor of all things. Nothing but the blood of Jesus Christ will cover me.

The Heartbeat of a Drum

I hear the sounds of a trumpet

The heartbeat of a drum

The claps of a people

Singing the praises of freedom

Shouting the joys of equality

Standing for harmony

Praying for the knowledge

I heard the sounds of misery

The beat of a drum

Cries of a people

A sad voice that hums

Moaning the pains of bondage

Yelling the sorrows of depression

Sitting in hell

Praying for the knowledge

I hear the sounds of a trumpet

The beat of a drum

Sounds of wings

Voices that hum

Singing the praises of freedom

Master! No more tears for me

Shouting the joys of heaven

Standing for harmony

Receiving the knowledge

Eternally

My Mind and the Mind of God

Let's look at the situation in the Garden of Eden. The devil let his pride get in the way of having a good relationship with God. A thought entered into his mind, and he actually thought that he was better than the Creator. Because of his mindset he was casted out of heaven, and became an enemy of God. With the same mind set the devil deceived the woman called Eve. Let us look at Genesis chapter three. It says that the snake was very crafty. It says "You will surely not die" the serpent said to the woman. "For God knows that when you eat from it your eyes will be opened, and you will be like God, knowing good from evil." (Genesis 3:4)

Can you count how many times a day you had thoughts? It would be totally impossible to count every thought that you had in one day. With a mind made in the likeness of God we are able to achieve many things. Just think about that for a minute. We are made in the image of God, and we are in His likeness. God is Omnipotent, and we carry some of his power. Therefore we are able to take on the likeness of God's mind. When we change our mindset in the likeness of God we are able to look beyond all of the bad things that are happening in the world. I did not say that we were not going to wrestle with the enemy in our minds, but we can have control over every negative thought that enters into our mind.

Homeless

A man on the corner

Selling bread for a dime

Life is passing surely

He is running out of time

How sad is his heart

Card board box for a home

Many worlds apart

Standing alone

Often the tears flow

More than he can stand

In reality trouble lives on

For this homeless man

The child next door

Only thirteen years of age

Suffers from hunger

Her mind is a deadly cage

No food to eat

The water well runs dry

She feels sadness and defeat
Her life is all a lie

How can one so young

Hurt so bad
She is not the only sad little girl

There are other homeless children in the world

Homeless

In the open

Running wild

Lonely sad

Rivers of Life

Lord from you flow the rivers of life
In you God we can trust
You are the great Jehovah God
You are the light of the world
In you God we can find rest
Our weary souls can find peace
With you Lord we have everything that we need
God I trust you
With all that I am
Because I have joy
I am glad
To call you my God
I am not ashamed to worship you Lord
I give myself to you Lord
O God of heavens and earth
Lord thank you
Thank you Lord
For being my God
You are so worthy
O great King
I thank you for all your love
God you are so good
You are the great I am
I will rejoice in you
Because you are God
Thank you Lord for all that you have done
I can depend on you
I love you Lord
No one can compare to you
You are the Great I Am
And Jehovah Yahweh

Jehovah

Lord as I look back on the week
I can say that I have been blessed
You O Lord have made a way for me
You have blessed my family
With all that we need
We have health, strength, and joy
You have made us well
We have all of our five senses
We have a nice place to stay
And we plenty of food to eat
Bless those Lord
Who have none?
Bless the single mother
That may not have food for her children
Bless the homeless man
Living in the alley
Bless that Father who has a sick son
I know that you are a healer Lord
You are Jehovah Nissi
You are my provider
You are El-Shaddai
The Prince of Peace
God you are the Great I am
You are The Most High God
You are Jehovah Shalom
And you are
Jehovah Shammah
I am a witness of your great works
You have saved me
And you have been my counsel
Thank Jehovah Rohi
You are my Shepard
I shall not want
God El-olam
You are the God of hosts
Jehovah Sabbaoth
As I reflect on this weekend I thank you Lord
For this day
You will always be worthy of my praise

Thank you Lord for all that you have done. This book is dedicated to all the single mothers and father that are raising their families. There are times when there is so much difficulty, and I am here to tell you that God is there to help you through.

God bless you always
Amanda Matthews